NATIONAL STRATEGY
for
COUNTERING
BIOLOGICAL THREATS

National Security Council

NOVEMBER 2009

THE WHITE HOUSE

WASHINGTON

November 23, 2009

My Fellow Americans,

Since the dawn of civilization, infectious diseases have shaped the course of human history. During the 20th century, we made remarkable progress in advancing public health, but in many ways we are currently more vulnerable than ever. Today, a tremendous interconnectedness brings the global community together and provides new opportunities for our mutual advancement. At the same time, however, it increases the potential for the spread of diseases such as H1N1 influenza and SARS which ignore geographic and political boundaries.

Advances within the life sciences hold extraordinary potential for beneficial progress, but they also can empower those who would use biological agents for ill purpose. Economic, political, and religious forces have given rise to a form of fanaticism that seeks to harm free societies. We know that some of these fanatics have expressed interest in developing and using biological weapons against us and our allies. Addressing these unique challenges requires a comprehensive approach that recognizes the importance of reducing threats from outbreaks of infectious disease whether natural, accidental, or deliberate in nature.

This *National Strategy for Countering Biological Threats* articulates our vision for managing these evolving and complex risks. It is a vision of shared commitment wherein the United States Government works with domestic and international partners to advance the health security of all people. It recognizes that the pace and progress of the life sciences require tailored approaches to mitigate the potential for misuse with minimal impacts upon beneficial use. Finally, it establishes a series of mutually reinforcing activities to address specific threats as they arise.

We will continue to face new and emerging biological threats that will require the coordinated and concerted efforts of a broad range of domestic and international partners. As we take action to counter these threats, we will work together to advance our own health security and provide for the improved condition of all humanity.

Contents

National Strategy for Countering Biological Threats

Introduction

We are experiencing an unparalleled period of advancement and innovation in the life sciences globally that continues to transform our way of life. Whether augmenting our ability to provide health care and protect the environment, or expanding our capacity for energy and agricultural production towards global sustainability, continued research and development in the life sciences is essential to a brighter future for all people.

The beneficial nature of life science research is reflected in the widespread manner in which it occurs. From cutting-edge academic institutes, to industrial research centers, to private laboratories in basements and garages, progress is increasingly driven by innovation and open access to the insights and materials needed to advance individual initiatives.

We must support the ongoing revolution in the life sciences by seeking to ensure that resulting discoveries and their applications, used solely for peaceful and beneficial purposes, are globally available. At the same time, we must be mindful of the risks throughout history posed by those who sought to misuse the products of new technologies for harmful purposes. Specifically, we must reduce the risk that misuse of the life sciences could result in the deliberate or inadvertent release of biological material in a manner that sickens or kills people, animals, or plants, or renders unusable critical resources.

The effective dissemination of a lethal biological agent within an unprotected population could place at risk the lives of hundreds of thousands of people. The unmitigated consequences of such an event could overwhelm our public health capabilities, potentially causing an untold number of deaths. The economic cost could exceed one trillion dollars for each such incident. In addition, there could be significant societal and political consequences that would derive from the incident's direct impact on our way of life and the public's trust in government.

Since 2001, the United States Government has significantly expanded its efforts to improve the Nation's ability to recognize and respond to acts of bioterrorism or other significant outbreaks of infectious disease; however, efforts targeted to prevent such threats have received comparatively limited policy focus or substantive guidance at the National level. Although it is entirely feasible to mitigate the impact of even a large-scale biological attack upon a city's population, doing so incurs a significant cost and effort. We therefore need to place increased priority on actions to further reduce the likelihood that such an attack might occur.

This *Strategy* will guide our efforts to prevent such incidents by reducing the risk that misuse of the life sciences or derivative materials, techniques, or expertise will result in the use or intent to use biological agents to cause harm. It also complements existing policies, plans, and preparations to advance our ability to respond to public health crises of natural, accidental, or deliberate origin.

Biological Threat Challenges

Biological weapons and their use or proliferation by States or non-State actors (biological threats) present a significant challenge to our national security. The development and use of biological weapons involves the diversion of resources that are globally available. Distinguishing illicit intent within the expanse of legitimate activity presents a unique challenge. It is quite possible that we would not obtain specific warning of an imminent threat or impending attack in time to stop it.

Despite the challenge of identifying and characterizing current and active biological threats, there is extensive documentation of a number of past activities that suggests the nature of the threat continues to evolve:

- From the end of World War II until the 1980s the principal threat has been from state-run programs. Fortunately, arsenals built under these programs were never unleashed and—thanks to significant investments and international cooperation over nearly two decades—the threat from several such programs has been reduced.

- In the last two decades, bioterrorism has emerged as another serious threat. In the 1980s, the United States had its first bioterrorist attack when the Rajneeshee cult contaminated salad bars with *Salmonella typhimurium* in a politically motivated attack that sickened hundreds, but fortunately, did not result in any loss of life.

- In the 1990s, the apocalyptic Aum Shinrikyo cult sprayed a liquid containing *Bacillus anthracis* (anthrax) spores from the roof of their headquarters near Tokyo, Japan. Once again, there was no loss of life as the strain of the bacteria used by the cult was not pathogenic.

- In 2001, letters containing anthrax spores were distributed via the United States postal system, infecting 22 people and resulting in 5 deaths, extensive social disruption, and enormous costs for emergency response and remediation.

- Also in 2001, while engaging the Taliban in Afghanistan, coalition forces came into possession of a significant body of evidence that al-Qa'ida was seeking to develop the capability to conduct biological weapons attacks. Although al-Qa'ida has lost many of the resources it had compiled prior to September 2001, it is prudent to assume that its intent to pursue biological weapons still exists.

We are fortunate that biological threats have not yet resulted in a catastrophic attack or accidental release in the United States. However, we recognize that: (1) the risk is evolving in unpredictable ways; (2) advances in the enabling technologies will continue to be globally available; and (3) the ability to exploit such advances will become increasingly accessible to those with ill intent as the barriers of technical expertise and monetary costs decline. Accordingly, we cannot be complacent but instead must take action to ensure that advances in the life sciences positively affect people of all nations while we reduce the risks posed by their misuse.

The *National Strategy for Countering Biological Threats*

Reducing the risks presented by the deliberate or accidental release of a biological agent requires the use of all instruments of national power, close coordination among all sectors of government, and effective partnerships among public and private institutions both nationally and internationally. Under the *National Strategy for Countering Biological Threats (Strategy)*, we will encourage the alignment of global attitudes against the intentional misuse of the life sciences or derivative materials, techniques, or expertise to harm people, agriculture, or other critical resources.

Our *Strategy* is targeted to reduce biological threats by: (1) improving global access to the life sciences to combat infectious disease regardless of its cause; (2) establishing and reinforcing norms against the misuse of the life sciences; and (3) instituting a suite of coordinated activities that collectively will help influence, identify, inhibit, and/or interdict those who seek to misuse the life sciences.

The *Strategy* provides a framework for future United States Government planning efforts that supports the overall *National Biodefense Strategy* (Homeland Security Presidential Directive (HSPD)-10/National Security Presidential Directive-33), and complements existing White House strategies related to biological threat preparedness and response:

- *Management of Domestic Incidents* (HSPD-5) and the related *National Response Framework*;

- *National Preparedness* (HSPD-8);

- *National Strategy for Defense of United States Agriculture and Food* (HSPD-9);

- *Medical Countermeasures against Weapons of Mass Destruction* (HSPD-18); and

- *Public Health and Medical Preparedness* (HSPD-21).

This *Strategy* reflects the fact that the challenges presented by biological threats cannot be addressed by the Federal Government alone, and that planning and participation must include the full range of domestic and international partners. It is guided by the following assumptions:

- Advances in the life sciences solely used in a peaceful and beneficial manner should globally available;

- A biological incident that results in mass casualties anywhere in the world increases the risk to all nations from biological threats;

- Biological attacks against animals or crops threaten food supplies and economic prosperity, potentially exacerbating broader security concerns and the global economy;

- Governmental, societal, organizational, and personal perceptions as to the legitimacy and efficacy of biological weapons can have an important impact upon the risk;

- It may not be possible to prevent all attacks; however, a coordinated series of actions can help to reduce the risk;

- A comprehensive and integrated approach is needed to prevent the full spectrum of biological threats as actions will vary in their effectiveness against specific threats; and

- The rapid detection and containment of, and response to, serious infectious disease outbreaks—whether of natural, accidental, or deliberate origin—advances both the health of populations and the security interests of States.

Objectives of the *Strategy*

Our *Strategy* addresses the full spectrum of opportunities for risk management that link, for example, a rural clinic overseas to a cutting-edge laboratory in America. Although the local circumstances in these environments are unique, our objectives will remain relevant to achieving our goal: **PROTECT** against the misuse of the life sciences to develop or use biological agents to cause harm. The objectives of our *Strategy* are:

- **Promote global health security:** Activities that should be taken to increase the availability of and access to knowledge and products of the life sciences that can help reduce impacts of outbreaks of infectious disease whether of natural, accidental, or deliberate origin.

- **Reinforce norms of safe and responsible conduct:** Activities that should be taken to reinforce a culture of responsibility, awareness, and vigilance among all who utilize and benefit from the life sciences to ensure that they are not diverted to harmful purposes.

- **Obtain timely and accurate insight on current and emerging risks:** Activities that serve to improve threat identification, notification, and assessment capabilities as well as our understanding as to the global progress and presence of the life sciences to help identify and understand new and emerging challenges and inform appropriate actions to manage the evolving risk.

- **Take reasonable steps to reduce the potential for exploitation:** Activities that are targeted to identify, sensitize, support, or otherwise safeguard knowledge and capabilities in the life sciences and related communities that could be vulnerable to accidents or misuse.

- **Expand our capability to prevent, attribute, and apprehend:** Activities that are intended to further hone the Nation's ability to identify and stop those with ill intent to reduce the risk of single, multiple, or sequential attacks.

- **Communicate effectively with all stakeholders:** Activities that should be conducted to ensure the Federal Government is advancing cogent, coherent, and coordinated messages.

- **Transform the international dialogue on biological threats:** Activities targeted to promote a robust and sustained discussion among all nations as to the evolving biological threat and identify mutually agreed steps to counter it.

Implementation of the Strategy

This *Strategy* outlines the Federal Government's approach to reducing the risks of biological weapons proliferation and terrorism. While this *Strategy* provides strategic guidance for the departments and agencies of the United States Government, it does not articulate or assign specific responsibilities to

Federal Departments and Agencies. The implementation of this *Strategy*, specific actions to be taken by Federal entities, and their specific measures of performance and effectiveness will be directed separately.

We are in the midst of a global revolution in the life sciences that will progress for at least the next few decades. As such, many of the objectives and courses of action outlined herein: (1) will take years to implement fully; (2) will need to be revisited and potentially revised to complement the evolving risk; and (3) will require the long-term sustainment of efforts among the full range of domestic and international partners and stakeholders.

The ongoing revolution in the life sciences already is a global endeavor. Broad access to life science findings and products ultimately will provide the tools and capabilities needed to manage the risk of accidents or misuse. Efforts to restrict or control the enabling materials and knowledge, while helpful in specific contexts, must be carefully defined and targeted.

We will continue to uphold our obligation under the Convention on the Prohibition of the Development, Production, and Stockpiling of Bacteriological (Biological) and Toxin Weapons and on Their Destruction (BWC) not in any way to "assist, encourage, or induce" any State, group of States, or international organizations to acquire biological weapons. Consistent with this and other obligations under domestic law and international agreements, we will seek to pursue policies and actions that promote the global availability of life science discoveries and technologies for peaceful purposes.

Objective One: Promote global health security

Many nations struggle daily to address the impact of naturally occurring infectious disease within their borders. In the face of this challenge, it can be difficult to find consensus on the need to address the risk from accidents or deliberate incidents.

In partnership with other nations, and consistent with international obligations, we will seek to advance access to and effective use of technologies to mitigate the impact from outbreaks of infectious disease, regardless of their cause. As more nations are better able to mitigate this impact, we expect that they may be better positioned to discuss—and take action to prevent—the risks associated with misuse.

Building Global Capacity for Disease Surveillance, Detection, Diagnosis, and Reporting

Ensuring the global availability of life science-enabled capabilities—such as disease surveillance and detection—to mitigate the risks from natural, accidental, and deliberate outbreaks directly enables progress on all three. We will work with partner countries and regions to assist in their efforts to comply with the World Health Organization's (WHO) International Health Regulations (IHR) as well as the World Organization of Animal Health's (OIE) and the United Nations Food and Agricultural Organization's (FAO) reporting guidelines in a manner that:

- Permits them to detect, identify, and report promptly any public, animal, or plant health or agricultural emergencies of international concern;

- Focuses on major population centers, known locations of endemic and epidemic disease and their vectors, and any known associated local terrorist or criminal threats;

- Is integrated and interoperable with their existing logistical infrastructure and sensitive to their public and agricultural health priorities;

- Is sustainable within the often limited resources of the country/region, either unilaterally or with other partners;

- Improves coordination between human, plant, and veterinary disease reporting systems, especially in relation to zoonotic diseases; and

- Is transparent and enables the sharing of information with international human, plant, and animal health agencies and the United States.

Improving International Capacity against Infectious Diseases

Ensuring that communities can quickly and effectively respond to large outbreaks of infectious disease in a manner that greatly reduces their impact is among the most effective ways to deter a deliberate attack and to minimize the consequences should an attack occur. In today's interconnected world, an outbreak of highly communicable disease anywhere on the globe increases the risk to everyone, particularly if that outbreak is of deliberate origin. Accordingly, we will continue to build upon bilateral and multilateral partnerships to improve international preparedness and global resilience against potentially catastrophic outbreaks of infectious disease by:

- Supporting efforts of partner countries and regions to advance the capability of medical, public health, agricultural, and veterinary systems to respond to and recover from disease outbreaks of any origin;

- Facilitating efforts of partner countries and regions to develop and exercise plans for responding to and recovering from large outbreaks of infectious diseases;

- Exploring opportunities with partner countries and regions to conduct joint development and procurement of medical countermeasures;

- Working with partner countries and regions to articulate and exercise plans in the event that we could contribute to their consequence management efforts;

- Sharing best practices and lessons learned from our domestic resilience activities through exchanges, joint exercises, and training; and

- Engaging international partners to optimize biological threat identification, assessment, and response through efforts to develop capabilities to conduct joint criminal and epidemiological investigations.

Objective Two: Reinforce norms of safe and responsible conduct

Through the course of its advancement, the ongoing life sciences revolution will continue to place significant capabilities in the hands of an ever increasing number of individuals. The intent underlying how these capabilities are used will determine the extent to which people benefit from them or experience the consequences of their misuse. Accordingly, we will advance and reinforce as a norm for the safe and beneficial use of the life sciences the exhortation of the BWC that their use as weapons would be "repugnant to the conscience of mankind."

Supporting the 'culture of responsibility' in the life sciences

Life scientists are best positioned to develop, document, and reinforce norms regarding the beneficial intent of their contribution to the global community as well as those activities that are fundamentally intolerable. Although other communities can make meaningful contributions, only the concerted and deliberate effort of distinguished and respected life scientists to develop, document, and ultimately promulgate such norms will enable them to be fully endorsed by their peers and colleagues. We will seek to facilitate these efforts by:

- Encouraging the constituencies of the global life sciences community to engage in a robust and sustained dialogue as to the development of behavioral norms and options for their codification;

- Encouraging professional societies in the life sciences to develop and communicate codes of ethics and consider how their membership policies can best reflect community norms;

- Assisting professional societies and other representatives of the life sciences community in the development of relevant educational and training materials;

- Ensuring the availability of tools and resources needed to document, communicate, and reinforce norms during the education and throughout the career of life scientists in academia, industry, or government; and

- Supporting efforts by life scientists to explore community-based approaches for identifying and addressing irresponsible conduct.

Advancing societal norms through legal mechanisms

Nations convey and reinforce behavioral norms within their civil society through a variety of means, including civil and criminal statutes, regulations, guidance, proclamations, or edicts. These items communicate standards of behavior for citizens along with an awareness of penalties associated with their violation and, when available, advice and recommendations for conducting positive and productive activities. Although such tools do not eliminate the potential for illicit behavior, their routine and regular enforcement help deter violation by the vast majority of people. We will seek to promote the use of such tools at home and encourage their development abroad by:

- Periodically reviewing, and as necessary, recommending updates to criminal statutes to ensure that they are well suited to the evolving risks of misuse of the life sciences;

- Ensuring members of stakeholder communities at unique risk of exploitation have access to guidance regarding actions that can reduce the risk of misuse;

- Supporting efforts of partner countries and regions to establish and build capacity to effectively implement legislation criminalizing the development and/or use of biological weapons and/ or acts of bioterrorism; and

- Engaging international partners and nongovernmental entities under existing obligations— such as the BWC and United Nations Security Council Resolution 1540—and via existing multilateral fora—such as the Australia Group and the G-8 Global Partnership—to develop and promulgate common standards, guidance, and best practices for actions relevant to preventing illicit use.

Objective Three: Obtain timely and accurate insight on current and emerging risks

Reducing the risks presented by those who seek to misuse the life sciences requires our continuing insight and thorough understanding of: advances in the life sciences; their global availability and use; naturally occurring infectious diseases in people, animals, and plants; global medical and public health capabilities and capacities; and specific efforts by those with ill intent to subvert resources available to them. Much of the information needed to provide situational awareness is derived from social networks within distinct and disparate communities. We will emphasize the need for each of these groups to enrich and expand their networks and ability to share data in a manner that appropriately protects individuals' privacy and other relevant sensitivities.

Staying abreast of the life sciences revolution

Advances in the life sciences are progressing globally at an unprecedented rate. The vast majority of this activity is wholly beneficial and poses little to no risk of misuse. Select findings and technologies however—such as the ability of techniques used for synthetic genomics to enable the *de novo* synthesis of certain high-risk pathogens and toxins—raise questions as to how we can best manage the risk while minimizing the impact on legitimate science. Accordingly, we will ensure that our policies and activities are fully informed by a robust and current awareness of advances in the life sciences and their potential impact upon the risk by:

- Ensuring appropriate Federal investments in "technology watch" initiatives that provide cutting edge insight and analysis from those currently engaged in the science;

- Encouraging the broad distribution of technology watch findings to those engaged in risk management activities across the Federal Government and appropriate nongovernmental partners;

- Reviewing and, as appropriate, updating our regulatory requirements and guidance on export controls to reflect the current state of the life sciences;

- Promoting the continued expansion of opportunities for employment within the Federal Government for those with life science expertise; and

- Ensuring life scientists employed by the Federal Government have access to necessary educational resources to maintain technical currency in appropriate departments and agencies.

Building knowledge as to the global disease burden and technological capabilities

A robust understanding of the nature, prevalence, and severity of infectious diseases both at home and abroad is critical for effective decisions for prevention, protection, preparedness, and response. In addition, a clear understanding of scientific capabilities and medical, veterinary, and public as well as agricultural health capacity abroad is essential to inform decisions on policies, programs, and investments that can best manage current and emerging risks. We will encourage the constituencies that comprise our scientific, agricultural, medical, and global public health communities to expand and strengthen their individual networks and improve our knowledge of global capabilities and needs to manage risks from naturally occurring and deliberately introduced infectious diseases by:

- Supporting efforts in partner countries and regions to develop mechanisms and capabilities for reporting to the WHO, OIE, FAO, and other partners validated data on human, animal, and plant outbreaks of infectious disease;

- Engaging Federal, nongovernmental, and international partners to advance awareness and understanding of global outbreaks of infectious disease;

- Engaging Federal, nongovernmental, and international partners to promote greater awareness and understanding of the global availability of and access to life sciences technologies and materials; and

- Promoting the development and use of mechanisms for reporting, preserving, and—as appropriate to improve transparency in government—sharing data on Federal programs and investments in international scientific, agricultural, medical, and public health collaborations.

Improving intelligence on deliberate biological threats

Timely and accurate information as to the capabilities and intent of those who seek to subvert the life sciences is exceptionally difficult to obtain. The intelligence community (IC), in collaboration with the broader United States Government and life science communities, must seek to close the gaps in our nation's intelligence collection and analytic capabilities directed at countering biological threats. The dynamic and evolving nature of the life sciences and potential threats will demand a detailed approach that yields actionable intelligence for all consumers. We will seek to meet this challenge by:

- Defining, integrating, focusing, and enhancing existing IC capabilities dedicated to current and strategic biological threats, whether from states, groups, or individuals;

- Ensuring the prioritization and sustained commitment of personnel and resources needed to optimize the IC's targeting, collection, analytic, and technological capabilities directed against biological threats;

- Advancing partnerships between the IC and non-IC departments and agencies in assessing potential threats and the risks from the intentional use of biological agents;

- Expanding the IC's support to non-IC departments and agencies and organizations at the Federal, State, local, and tribal level regarding actionable intelligence on biological threats; and

- Evaluating on a regular basis the IC's efforts and progress on understanding and countering biological threats.

Facilitating data sharing and knowledge discovery

Improving our access to the above sources of information will provide little benefit unless we can enable the various communities to share information in a manner that yields meaningful discoveries while protecting sensitive privacy, security, and proprietary data. We will seek to do this by:

- Developing a strategy for advancing situational awareness and a plan that identifies key elements of information to be shared, critical sensitivities to be protected, and a framework for enabling information exchange;

- Fostering information sharing between public health, law enforcement and security, intelligence, and the life sciences community to identify potential threats, reduce vulnerabilities, and improve response activities and investigations of suspected biological incidents; and

- Evaluating the role for novel technologies in facilitating intradepartmental, interdepartmental, and open sharing of information in a manner that protects those elements deemed critically sensitive.

Objective Four: Take reasonable steps to reduce the potential for exploitation

To present a credible biological threat, those with the intent to do harm must have access to relevant expertise, information, and material. There is no feasible or effective process that can restrict access to the full range of life science resources that could contribute to misuse. Actions to identify specific risks and protect relevant materials, items, and technologies can, however, increase both our chances of detecting illicit activity and the costs and effort for such activity without having serious consequences upon the pace and progress of legitimate life science activities.

Managing risks posed by dual-use information of concern

Some of the information derived from the life sciences is referred to as "dual-use" due to its potential for misuse to cause harm. Certain pieces of this information of concern can be uniquely helpful in permitting those with ill intent to present a biological threat. It is important for those who routinely access and utilize such information to be aware of its potential for harm and ensure that it is responsibly used. We will seek to address risks posed by dual-use information of concern by:

- Providing detailed guidelines that can aid in the identification of such information and enable actions that reduce the potential for its misuse while recognizing the importance of legitimate use;

- Encouraging activities by academia and the private sector to develop community-based mechanisms for sharing experiences and best practices for risk management;

- Promoting discussions among U.S. scientific experts and their international colleagues to raise awareness of the risk and advance thoughts on how best to address it; and

- Enabling efforts by the life sciences community to incorporate guidance and best practices into education and training materials.

Optimizing security of known virulent high-risk pathogens and toxins

Among the microbial organisms capable of causing disease, there are a relatively small number of high-risk pathogens and toxins that have properties which enable them to be used in a deliberate attack. Nearly all such pathogens and toxins are naturally occurring and can be found in and isolated from environmental sources around the globe. As such, it is impossible to eliminate the risk posed by deliberate use of these pathogens and toxins; however, it is reasonable to seek to reduce the risk by limiting ready access to known virulent strains of high-risk pathogens and toxins. In addition, the use of proper safety controls and practices is a key contributor to risk management. Our efforts in this area will focus on:

- Optimizing our domestic laws, regulations, policies and practices for securing high-risk pathogens and toxins and providing detailed guidance for improved compliance;

- Improving use of mechanisms to report theft or loss or release from laboratories holding dangerous pathogens and toxins to appropriate public health and law enforcement agencies;

- Supporting the efforts of partner countries and regions to ensure the application of biological security and safety practices in a risk-based and sustainable manner;

- Maintaining and further promulgating guidance on the use of best practices, safety equipment, and facility engineering controls for biological safety when working with high-risk pathogens and toxins;

- Promoting the development of international guidelines for safety and security of high-risk pathogens and toxins and their broadest possible adoption; and

- Working with partner countries and regions to identify collections of high-risk pathogens and toxins, and where possible, consolidate collections at national regional centers of excellence, keeping in mind the need to be able to comply with the WHO's IHR and OIE guidelines.

Addressing emerging technology-enabled risks

As our awareness of advances in the life sciences expands, we may identify novel or emerging capabilities that impact the risk. We will engage experts in our efforts to evaluate the likely impact upon risk and the benefits and costs of potential mitigative actions in a manner that seeks to appropriately balance the potential for managing the risk with the potential for beneficial use. We will provide clear guidance to facilitate compliance with any such mitigative actions.

Objective Five: Expand our capability to prevent, attribute, and apprehend

No matter how effective our efforts to increase the barriers and reduce the perceived benefits to development and/or use of biological weapons, we cannot eliminate the possibility that some may seek to misuse the life sciences to do harm. Also, because biological threats by their nature lend themselves to permitting an aggressor to conduct multiple attacks in different areas, either simultaneously or in sequence, our timely recognition and apprehension of the perpetrator is critical to reducing the risk of follow-on attacks. We must ensure that law enforcement, national security, and homeland security communities have access to the full range of tools and capabilities needed to identify and disrupt the efforts of those with ill intent—preferably before they have the opportunity to conduct an attack—and apprehend and successfully prosecute all offenders.

Ensuring robust capabilities for law enforcement and security

Our law enforcement and homeland security communities are a critical front line in recognizing, preventing, and responding to the entire spectrum of illicit activities involving the life sciences or derivative materials, techniques, or expertise. Whether the offender is seeking to poison someone or is part of a group that intends to contaminate a wide metropolitan area, Federal, State, local, and tribal law enforcement and security officials must be well positioned to receive and respond to tips, safely and successfully handle potentially contaminated material, conduct investigations, and prosecute perpetrators and facilitators. We will seek to prepare those responsible for our security to address biological threats by:

- Establishing processes for sharing data and expertise on biological threats among Federal, State, local, and tribal law enforcement, health, and security communities;

- Providing training for law enforcement, health, and security personnel on recognizing and responding to situations involving potential biological threats, including performing joint criminal and epidemiological investigations;

- Ensuring our law enforcement and security personnel have tailored tactics, techniques, and procedures and access to the tools needed to respond to biological threats; and

- Promoting bilateral and multilateral discussions with those from international law enforcement and security communities to improve information sharing on threats and best practices.

Empowering an informed, involved, and observant citizenry

Individual members of our communities are best positioned to observe the initial indicators of illicit activity. It is critical that these individuals are willing and able to inform law enforcement and security communities of suspicious or unusual activity. We must seek to encourage the development of social networks that derive from positive and productive relationships among our law enforcement and security communities and members of those communities at unique risk of exploitation. We will seek to foster these relationships by:

- Identifying and articulating our rationale for particular communities at heightened risk of exploitation;

- Conducting outreach from law enforcement and security community professionals to willing representatives of the identified communities to discuss the risks;

- Engaging members of the vulnerable community to raise awareness of the types of activities that would reasonably be considered unusual or suspicious; and

- Establishing mechanisms for willing members of the vulnerable community to notify appropriate authorities of unusual or suspicious activities in a confidential manner.

Ensuring robust capabilities to disrupt or interdict illicit activity

Where we identify States, groups, or individuals seeking to acquire or use biological weapons, we will use all appropriate means to disrupt or deny their efforts, drawing on a wide range of counterterrorism, counterproliferation, intelligence, law enforcement, and other tools.

Developing effective interdiction capabilities, both ourselves and in concert with partner nations, can contribute to our efforts to counter or deter those who seek to transfer, acquire, develop, or use a biological weapon. Effective interdiction capabilities also can help deter those who otherwise would consider providing materials, equipment, or assistance. For example, since 2003, more than 90 countries have endorsed the Proliferation Security Initiative (PSI) and thus committed to cooperating to interdict WMD-related shipments of proliferation concern to and from both States and non-State actors. We will continue to partner with other nations and advance our capabilities against biological threats by:

- Ensuring that our armed forces, law enforcement, and security communities have access to appropriate plans, procedures, and tools for effective and safe operations;

- Promoting the use of simulations among Federal partners to exercise our capabilities, refine operational concepts, and strengthen relationships across government; and

- Working with international partners through appropriate venues to promote appropriate communication, coordination, cooperation, and capacity building.

Enhancing microbial forensics and attribution

The primary objectives of any investigation into the alleged use, intended use, or development of a biological weapon are to prevent casualties, protect the public health, and attribute the activity to its perpetrator. Attribution of biological threats entails the analysis of data from a variety of sources, including technical information on samples containing biological material derived through microbial forensic analyses. We will seek to continue to advance our capabilities for attribution and microbial forensics by:

- Ensuring that law enforcement tactics, techniques, and procedures and public health and agricultural processes are coordinated and that the investigations are synergistic;

- Ensuring the availability of a detailed concept of operations for information sharing and all-source analysis to support timely attribution of biological incidents;

- Establishing a National-level research and development strategy and investment plan for advancing the field of microbial forensics; and

- Maintaining the National Biological Forensics Analysis Center as the Nation's lead Federal facility for forensic analysis of biological material in support of law enforcement investigations.

Objective Six: Communicate effectively with all stakeholders

Successful implementation of this *Strategy* requires the long term and concerted action of a broad range of stakeholders, most of whom are not part of the United States Government. As such, there are a number of activities that should be taken to ensure we advance cogent, coherent, and coordinated messages regarding our understanding of the threat, steps we are taking to reduce the risks, and capabilities that we can make available to help our colleagues manage the risks. We will seek to advance effective communications and increase transparency in our actions by:

- Ensuring that all Federal partners develop, utilize, and update tools for communicating with the full range of domestic and international stakeholders;

- Encouraging that—whenever possible—Federal departments and agencies coordinate their outreach efforts to include conducting joint or multi-partner activities;

- Promoting greater outreach and participation of Federal representatives in scientific, technical, academic, and other professional and public fora; and

- Establishing and maintaining an updated web-based portal that serves as the general point of entry for the public for information on the full range of our policies and activities related to risk management in the life sciences.

Objective Seven: Transform the international dialogue on biological threats

The life sciences revolution is global in nature and people of all nations can benefit from efforts to reduce the risk of misuse to enable biological threats. Optimal implementation of any effort to manage the risk requires international cooperation and coordination. Currently, the plurality of perspectives in the international community as to the severity of the risk and mitigative actions that nations should take presents a challenge to risk management. We will seek to advance the international dialogue by framing the risk in a broader context and seeking to identify helpful activities that nations can agree to undertake in a multilateral, bilateral, or unilateral manner even as varying perspectives on the immediacy of the risk may persist.

Revitalizing the Biological and Toxin Weapons Convention (BWC)

The BWC is a uniquely important venue through which we can promote and globally advance our objectives for non-proliferation and risk management of biological threats. The membership of the BWC, however, is not universal and concerns remain that some treaty partners may be developing biological weapons. As the central international forum dedicated to mitigating risks posed by the development and use of biological weapons, the BWC can help focus attention on the evolving nature of biological threats, increase attention to and promote international efforts to prevent proliferation and terrorism, and build tighter linkages between the health and security sectors. We will seek to utilize the BWC as our premiere forum for global outreach and coordination on the full scope of risk management activities by:

- Promoting confidence in effective BWC implementation and compliance by its States Parties, *inter alia*, by promoting transparency about legitimate activities and pursuing compliance diplomacy to address concerns;

- Promoting universal membership in the Convention;

- Ensuring that our participation in BWC meetings is broadly inclusive of relevant departments and agencies and headed by an appropriately senior representative;

- Advancing a substantive agenda that emphasizes topics and activities consistent with the objectives of this *Strategy* with broad potential to enhance global risk management;

- Seeking to renew existing relationships while building new, broader coalitions of "like-minded" BWC States Parties; and

- Encouraging stronger partnerships between security and public health communities by focusing on activities that improve global capabilities to counter infectious disease in a manner that mitigates risks from natural, accidental, and deliberate outbreaks.

Expanding our international partnerships and bioengagement

Over the past decade, our cooperative partnerships with a number of nations have demonstrably reduced the risks posed by legacy biological weapons programs. By assisting with efforts to redirect former weapons scientists, repurpose or decommission facilities and equipment, develop and implement practices that permit safe and secure work with high-risk pathogens and toxins, build scientific ties, and improve mutual understanding, our security engagement programs have developed a strong track record of effective risk management. We will seek to build upon this record by forging new partnerships that reduce the risks from biological threats by:

- Providing assistance to partner countries and regions along the spectrum of objectives in this *Strategy* in a manner that meets our partners' needs and is sustainable within the often limited resources of the countries and regions, either unilaterally or in partnership with others;

- Leveraging the best practices of our engagement programs while evolving and broadening the scope and nature of efforts in which we engage our international partners;

- Setting priorities and coordinating across United States Government assistance programs for bioengagement, including public health, nonproliferation, and S&T programs to ensure that efforts are appropriately targeted, mutually reinforcing, non-duplicative, and consistent with program mission and U.S. policy priorities; and

- Coordinating our biological security programs with our international partners in a manner that, wherever possible, sets mutual priorities for engagement.

Integrating efforts to meet our international obligations

We, and many of our international colleagues, have a number of multilateral and bilateral obligations that lie at the nexus of security, health, and science. We will continue to meet our obligations; however, we will look for opportunities to leverage synergies in activities that are relevant to multiple fora.

For example, whether we are: (1) responding to assistance requests for guidance on handling high-risk pathogens and toxins to enable partner countries to meet their obligations under United Nations Security Council Resolution 1540; (2) providing technical support to other countries to meet their disease surveillance and reporting obligations under the WHO's IHRs and OIE guidelines; (3) contributing technical assistance for securing high-risk pathogens and toxins in a partner country in accordance with Article X of the BWC; or (4) transferring material and equipment to permit, for example, a North Atlantic Treaty Organization ally to respond more effectively to a local outbreak of a high-risk pathogen, our efforts will reflect improved coordination and communication among Federal departments and agencies and with our international partners.

Roles and Responsibilities

Because of the broad-based and unique challenges presented by biological threats, responsibility for their prevention must involve all levels of government and include all segments of society, around the globe. No single stakeholder can fully address the challenge of biological threats on its own.

The Federal Government

Although the Federal Government plays a crucial role in framing and coordinating efforts to reduce the likelihood of biological threats, the success of this endeavor is largely dependent upon the activities of partners at the local and State levels and internationally. Specific Federal responsibilities include the following:

- Visibly complying with our obligations under the BWC, UNSCR 1540, WHO's IHR, OIE guidelines, the Global Health Security Initiative, the Australia Group, and other relevant bilateral and multilateral agreements;

- Advancing global situational awareness, disease surveillance, resilience, and other activities to counter specific threats from those who would seek to develop or use biological weapons;

- Ensuring that Federal Departments and Agencies have developed and are employing complementary and multi-layered systems for influencing, identifying, inhibiting, and interdicting those who would seek to develop or use biological weapons;

- Facilitating, through laws, regulations, guidance, and funding, State and local public health, agricultural, medical, clinical, and law enforcement efforts to secure and protect high-risk pathogens and toxins and recognize and respond to illicit biological activities;

- Providing guidance and, as appropriate, funding to the private sector to support awareness-raising, training, and appropriate public-private partnerships, in conjunction with states and localities; and

- Conducting the full range of preparations to ensure an effective response in the event of a biological incident.

States and Localities

Our communities, and particularly our medical, scientific, veterinary, agricultural, and security practitioners, are on the front lines in reducing the domestic risks posed by biological threats. We will encourage State and local governments to undertake the following:

- Establishing comprehensive capabilities—including coordination with appropriate Federal partners—for law enforcement professionals to recognize quickly and respond effectively to suspected activities involving the planned illicit use of biological material;

- Ensuring that all reasonable measures are taken to promote the safety and security of high-risk pathogens and toxins at facilities within their communities;

- Promoting a productive dialogue between the health, agriculture, and security sectors of the community; and

- Preparing now to ensure an effective response in the event of a biological incident.

The Private Sector

The private sector represents a unique and multifaceted component of our society because of the essential goods and services it provides and the capabilities it can bring to bear to mitigate the risks of exploitation. We will encourage the United States private sector to undertake the following:

- Conducting organizational assessments regarding potential vulnerabilities that could give aid to those seeking to develop or use biological weapons and taking all reasonable measures to reduce their risk of exploitation;

- Ensuring that all reasonable measures are taken to promote the safety and security of high-risk pathogens and toxins within their possession;

- Establishing and supporting robust participation in fora where sector colleagues and other stakeholders can discuss risks, raise awareness, and explore community-based approaches and best practices for risk management; and

- Maintaining productive working relationships with local, State, and Federal law enforcement agencies and reporting suspicious/illicit activities to appropriate authorities.

Individuals and Families

There is a critical role for families and individuals in reducing the risks from biological threats. Individual contributions to community resilience can undermine motivations for biological threats by reducing their effectiveness. We will encourage individuals and families to undertake the following:

- Following general guidance for disaster preparedness, such as keeping supplies of food and other materials at home—as recommended by authorities—to support essential needs of the household for several days if necessary;

- Being prepared to follow public health guidance that may include limiting their mobility throughout the community for several days or weeks, or utilizing designated evacuation routes; and

- Informing appropriate authorities when they encounter or observe suspicious or unusual activities.

International Partners

Our relationships with the United Nations, international organizations, foreign governments, and the private sector are critical to the success of our efforts and we will robustly engage them in multilateral and bilateral fora. Our coordination with the international community to counter biological threats is a core and cross-cutting element of our overall strategy. The tone, tenor, and quality of the United States Government's efforts and that of our international partners will be important to determine our mutual success. We will look to encourage our international partners to:

- Comply fully with their legal and politically-binding obligations under the BWC — for those that are not party to the BWC, we will encourage them to sign and ratify the Convention so that its principles can be a truly global norm;

- Advance policies and practices that establish and reinforce norms against the misuse of the knowledge and capabilities that arise from the life sciences while encouraging their free and open availability for peaceful and beneficial use;

- Place special emphasis on meeting their obligations under the WHO's IHR and OIE and FAO guidelines by establishing effective and sustainable systems for disease surveillance, detection, diagnosis, and reporting;

- Develop and employ complementary and multi-layered systems for influencing, identifying, inhibiting, and interdicting biological threats;

- Place priority on establishing effective and sustainable capabilities to respond to potentially catastrophic outbreaks of natural, accidental, or deliberate infectious disease within their borders and increase regional cooperation in consequence management;

- Engage in broad dialogue as to the perception of the spectrum of risks—current and future— enabled by the ongoing advances in the life sciences and helpful steps that can be taken towards risk management;

- Pursue bilateral and multilateral partnerships targeted to facilitate the efforts of partner nations to institute and implement laws, policies, and practices that collectively reduce the risks posed by misuse of the life sciences;

- Ensure the development and application of biological security and safety practices in a risk based and sustainable manner; and

- Continue to partner on PSI, the Australia Group, and other multilateral and bilateral initiatives to reduce the risk of biological weapons and other WMD threats.